Table of Contents

Introduction 3
    Nutritional Value Of Coffee 3
    Health Benefits Of Drinking Coffee 4
    Risks 7
    Coffee Machines And Brewing Techniques 9
Filter Drip Methods 10
    The Automatic Drip Method 11
    The Manual Drip Method 12
    The Cold-Press Method 14
    The French Press Method 17
    The Vacuum Pot Method 19
    The Middle Eastern Method 21
    The Percolator Method 24
    Tips For Making The Perfect Cup Of Coffee 25
Recipes 28
    Coffee Syrup 28
    Espresso Syrup 30
    Chocolate Syrup 30
    Vanilla Whipped Cream 32
    Espresso Whipped Cream 33
    Coffee Liqueur Whipped Cream 33
    Chocolate Whipped Cream 34

Coffee Whipped Cream 35
Soy Whipped Cream 36
Be Mine Latte 37
French Kiss Caffè Latte 38
Love Potion Latte 39
Irish Elixir Espresso 40
Iced Irish Coffee 41
Shamrock Shimmy (Nonskinny) Latte 41
Seven-Layer Latte 42
Thanksgiving Orange Latte 44
Pumpkin Cheesecake Latte 45
Happy Holiday Coffee Punch 46
Orange Yule Delight Latte 47
Christmas Cappuccino 48
Snowflake Latte 49
Classic Christmas Coffee 50
Candy Cane Latte 51
Midnight Star Coffee Cocktail 52

Introduction

When people think of coffee, they usually think of its ability to provide an energy boost. However, according to some research, it can also offer some other important health benefits, such as a lower risk of liver cancer, type 2 diabetes, and heart failure. Worldwide, experts estimate that people consume around 2.25 billion cups of coffee per day. Researchers have looked at the benefits of drinking coffee for conditions such as diabetes, cardiovascular disease, inflammatory bowel disease, and liver disease. There is evidence to support some, but not all, of these claims. Coffee contains a number of useful nutrients, including riboflavin (vitamin B-2), niacin (vitamin B-3), magnesium, potassium, and various phenolic compounds, or antioxidants. Some experts suggest that these and other ingredients in coffee can benefit the human body in various ways. This book looks at how to make coffee, the health benefits of drinking coffee, the evidence supporting those benefits, and the risks of drinking coffee.

Nutritional Value Of Coffee

Regular black coffee (without milk or cream) is low in calories. In fact, a typical cup of black coffee only contains around 2 calories. However, adding cream or sugar will increase the calorific value. Coffee beans also contain polyphenols, a type of antioxidant. Antioxidants can help rid the body of free radicals, a type of waste product that the body naturally produces as a result of certain processes. Free radicals are toxic and may cause inflammation. Scientists have found links between inflammation and various aspects of metabolic syndrome, including type 2 diabetes and obesity. In 2018, some researchers suggested that the antioxidant content of coffee may offer protection from metabolic syndrome. The author of one article from 2017 note that although scientists can prove that certain compounds are present in coffee beans, it remains unclear what happens to them once they enter the human body.

Health Benefits Of Drinking Coffee
Coffee and diabetes

Coffee may help protect against type 2 diabetes. In 2014, researchers who gathered data on over 48,000 people found that those who increased their coffee consumption by at least one cup per day over 4 years had an 11% lower risk of type 2 diabetes than those who did not increase their intake. A meta-analysis from 2017 concluded that people who drank four to six cups of either caffeinated or decaffeinated coffee each day appeared to have a lower risk of metabolic syndrome, including type 2 diabetes.

Coffee and Parkinson's disease

Various studies have shown that caffeine, which is present in coffee and many other beverages, may help protect against Parkinson's disease. One team concluded that men who drink over four cups of coffee per day might have a fivefold lower risk of Parkinson's than those who do not. In addition, the caffeine in coffee may help control movement in people with Parkinson's, according to one 2012 study. The findings of a 2017 meta-analysis suggested a link between coffee consumption and a lower risk of Parkinson's disease, even among people who smoke. This team also found that people who drink coffee may be less likely to experience depression and cognitive conditions such as Alzheimer's. There was not enough evidence to prove that drinking decaffeinated coffee would help prevent Parkinson's disease, however.

Coffee and liver cancer

Italian researchers found that coffee consumption lowers the risk of liver cancer by around 40%. Some of the results suggest that people who drink three cups per day might have a 50% lower risk. Also, a 2019 literature review concluded that "coffee intake probably reduce the risk of liver cancer."

Coffee and other liver diseases

A meta-analysis from 2017 concluded that consuming any type of coffee appeared to reduce the risk of liver cancer, nonalcoholic fatty liver disease, and cirrhosis. People who consume coffee may also have a lower risk of gallstone disease. In 2014, researchers looked at coffee consumption among people with primary sclerosing cholangitis (PSC) and primary biliary cirrhosis (PBC). These are autoimmune conditions that affect the bile ducts in the liver. They found that people with PSC were more likely to have a lower coffee intake than those without the condition. There was no evidence to suggest that coffee intake was different among people with or without PBC. Also, one 2014 study suggested a link between coffee consumption and a lower risk of dying from nonviral hepatitis-related cirrhosis. The researchers suggested that drinking two or more cups of coffee every day might reduce the risk by 66%.

Coffee and heart health

One 2012 study concluded that drinking coffee in moderation, or consuming around two 8-ounce servings per day, may protect against heart failure. People who drank moderate amounts of coffee each day had an 11% lower risk of heart failure than those who did not. One 2017 meta-analysis found that caffeine consumption may have at least a small benefit for cardiovascular health, including blood pressure. Some studies, however, found higher levels of blood lipids (fat) and cholesterol in people who consumed more coffee.

Risks

Drinking too much coffee can also have some adverse effects. In the sections below, we cover some of these risks.

Bone fractures

Some studies have found that women who drink a lot of coffee may have a higher risk of bone fractures. Men with a higher coffee intake, on the other hand, appear to have a slightly lower risk.

Pregnancy

The researchers added that coffee consumption may not be safe during pregnancy. In fact, there is some evidence to suggest a link between high coffee consumption and pregnancy loss, a low birth weight, and preterm birth.

Endometriosis

There may be a higher risk of endometriosis among women who drink coffee, but there is not enough evidence to confirm such a link.

Gastroesophageal reflux disease

People who drink a lot of coffee may have a slightly higher risk of this condition.

Anxiety

Consuming high amounts of caffeine may increase the risk of anxiety, especially among people with panic disorder or social anxiety disorder. Less commonly, it may trigger mania and psychosis in those who are susceptible.

Mental health

One study from 2016 concluded that a high intake of caffeine during adolescence can lead to permanent changes in the brain. The scientists behind the study expressed concern that this could increase the risk of anxiety-related conditions in adulthood.

Presence of toxic ingredients

In 2015, researchers found relatively high levels of mycotoxins in commercial coffee. Mycotoxins are toxic substances that can contaminate coffee as a natural product. Some people worry that acrymalide, another chemical present in coffee, may be dangerous.

Coffee Machines And Brewing Techniques
There are many ways to prepare a good cup of coffee. You'd be hard pressed (or perhaps French pressed!) to find a bad cup of joe these days. Whichever brewing style or tool is used, all methods have one thing in common: they all use hot water to extract the flavors and aromas from ground coffee beans. Personal taste dictates the strength or weakness of the coffee, as well as the method with which to make it. Each method offers different advantages and disadvantages, achieves a distinguished coffee character,

and attracts a different audience for reasons of culture, habit, taste, and/or lifestyle. Quality, convenience, simplicity, theatrics, or, perhaps, just plain passion also come into play. The following outlines the principal coffee-brewing machines and vessels to choose from. Please keep in mind, however, that besides the brewing method used, every finished coffee beverage will also differ greatly, based on the following factors:

• the kind of roasted coffee beans

• the amount and fineness of the coffee grind

Filter Drip Methods

Filter drip methods are the most widely used coffee-making techniques in North America and northern Europe. They permit the use of very fine coffee grinds for quick and thorough coffee extraction. Initially, a paper filter is placed in a plastic, glass, or ceramic holder. This filter holder sits on top of a flameproof glass carafe or coffeepot. Finely ground coffee is then placed in the filter. Boiling water is poured onto the ground coffee. The freshly brewed coffee then drips into the vessel below, while the grounds remain in the filter for easy disposal.

The Automatic Drip Method

The method

In an electric drip coffeemaker, place the ground coffee in a paper liner fitted inside the machine's cone-shaped or round filter. The hot water is heated automatically and drips through the coffee bed, trickling into a pot that sits on the machine's warming plate, known as "the burner."

Brewing tips

To prevent a burnt flavor, never keep the coffeepot on its electric burner for longer than 20 minutes. Keep the coffee warm, if necessary, in an insulated thermal carafe. Be sure to first preheat the carafe with hot tap water, so the cold glass lining inside the carafe does not cool down the fresh hot coffee. Transfer the finished coffee to the carafe immediately after it has been brewed. Blend the aromas of the finished coffee by swirling the coffee in the pot just prior to pouring the first cup.

Advantages

Set 'em and forget 'em! Automatic coffeemakers are ideal anytime you want a quick, convenient cup of coffee—especially first thing in the morning! This is the best way to make coffee for a crowd. Easy cleanup—the paper filters can be disposed of easily (if you compost, toss them into the mix). A reusable wire mesh filter, often sold separately by the coffeemaker's manufacturer, may be used as an environmentally friendly alternative to disposable paper filters. A halfway measure would be to buy only unbleached paper filters.

Disadvantages

Paper filters can absorb some of the coffee's flavor, and white paper filters have been processed with bleach. A burnt, slightly bitter taste results when a pot of coffee remains on the machine's electrified burner too long (20 minutes or longer). Overheating it throws the finished flavor of the coffee out of balance. Some coffee drinkers seeking to lead a more environmentally friendly life would prefer not to use electrical power to obtain their brew.

The Manual Drip Method
The method

Place the ground coffee in the paper or wire mesh filter that is designed to fit in a wedge-shaped filter holder whose flat base sits upon a carafe or heat-resistant cup or mug. Heat the water to boiling in a kettle. Allow the boiled water to rest for 10 to 15 seconds, then pour it slowly onto the ground coffee in the filter holder. The coffee will then drip into your container of choice. The best-known brands of this device are Melitta and Chemex.

Brewing tips

Be sure to preheat the container gently by rinsing it with hot (not boiling) tap water before filtering the coffee into it. Once the water has boiled, let it rest for 10 to 15 seconds before pouring it onto the ground coffee in the cone-shaped filter. Premoisten the ground coffee by initially pouring a little hot water over it, wetting it evenly. For example: If 1/2 cup (125 ml) of ground coffee is used, dampen it with ½ cup (125 ml) of hot water. Wait 30 seconds before pouring the remaining 2 1/2 cups (625 ml) of water through. The initial contact of water with the ground coffee releases a concentration of delicate coffee aromas and flavors. The premoistened ground coffee creates a smaller, denser volume packed into the deep bed, which enables the hot water to flow through them evenly.

Advantages

Portion and waste control are benefits of this method, if only one to three cups are required. Complete control of coffee-to-water ratio and water temperature ensures a better-quality coffee than does the automatic drip method. The coffee flavors are not burnt or destroyed, as in the automatic method, where the coffee carafe is left sitting on a heated burner. This method is portable—great for camping!

Disadvantages

More time and attention is required for this method (however, a better quality of coffee is guaranteed), since one must boil water separately, then manually pour the water through the coffee in the filter. Careless pouring may result in a brew speckled with grounds.

The Cold-Press Method

This coffee-brewing technique creates a cold coffee concentrate. My sister, Sonia, introduced me to this method back in 1994. I'll never forget that cold-pressed and very passionate coffee experience—when she showed me her cold carafe "in process and purpose" in her fridge.

The method

The actual brewing container for this method is a big white plastic form fitted with a filter. The recommended cold-press coffee-making containers of choice are called the Toddy Method, and there is also one called the Filtron Coffee System. Fill the brewing container with 1 pound of medium-ground coffee. Pour 4 cups of cold water over the coffee in the filter. Wait for 5 minutes—DO NOT STIR. Then slowly and evenly add 5 more cups of cold water. Again, DO NOT STIR. Place the container in the refrigerator. Allow 10 to 12 hours for the coffee to steep through the "Toddy," or coldpress filter. The liquid coffee will drain through the filter into a glass carafe. When the cold-filtering process has been completed, store the finished concentrate in the sealed glass decanter it has trickled into, and keep it tightly capped and refrigerated until use. This method yields 9 cups of cold coffee concentrate.

Brewing tips

Hot Coffee: To microwave, add 1 part concentrate to 3 parts cold water, then heat. Or add 1 part concentrate to a container of kettle-boiled hot water. Cold/Iced Coffee: This is the premier method of making iced coffee because it blends so well. Add 1 part concentrate to 2 parts water, over ice. Cold coffee brewed this way makes great coffee ice cubes, too.

Advantages

According to Toddy Coffee Makers, their cold brew system produces 67 percent less acid than does coffee made by conventional hot-water methods. Cold-brewed coffee is believed to have approximately 33 percent less caffeine than hot water methods. (As reported by MSNBC.) It's great for iced coffee recipes, coffeehouses, and iced drink–lovers. Add ice to the cold-press brew and you're done! This method is great for camping coffee. Simply add campfire-heated water to your coffee concentrate.

Disadvantages

The flavors of the cold-press method are weaker and less interesting to the French press and espresso enthusiasts (those techniques follow). If you normally make 1 cup to 3 cups of coffee at a time, the cold-press method may not be appropriate, as this method works best with a full pound of coffee, which produces more concentrate than you may desire to store in the fridge.

The French Press Method

The French press, or plunger-pot, method is easy to master and produces an extremely rich, robust coffee. It is the next best brew to espresso. The ground coffee directly infuses with slightly cooled boiling water, creating a promising marriage of flavor and aroma.

The method

Prewarm the glass beaker by rinsing it with hot water. Place the preferred amount of coffee in the beaker and fill with slightly cooled boiling water. Place the plunger lid on the beaker. The coffee should be allowed to steep for 4 to 6 minutes, then the meshed plunger lid should be pressed down gently through the coffee suspension. This separates the finished coffee from the grounds, which are pressed, or plunged, down to the bottom of the pot.

Brewing tips

Measure 2 level tablespoons (30 ml) of ground coffee for every 6 ounces (170 ml) of water. Water selection is also key. The higher the quality of the water used, the better your coffee will taste. Prerinse the glass plunger pot with hot (not boiling) water; add the slightly cooled (approximately 212°F [100°C]) kettle-boiled water to the ground coffee, then wrap a terrycloth towel around the pot during steeping. This will keep the finished coffee hot longer.

Advantages

This method guarantees the richest body of coffee (if done properly), except for espresso. The steeping time is less than that of drip methods. The pressure application is slight; the water is hotter; the ratio of coffee to water is higher. The ground coffee steeps in water just under the boiling point, with no further boiling or burning, preserving the dark, delightful coffee aroma and flavor without a trace of bitterness. The delicate aroma of the coffee oils are not removed by a paper filter. This method is quick and it is also portable. The plunger pot can double as a milk frother to make cappuccinos and lattes! Heat a cup of milk (nonfat milk works best), or soy or rice milk, in a saucepan on the stove, or in a microwave. Do not overheat or scald the milk. It should be heated just until it is too hot to put your finger into it. Pour the milk into a clean, rinsed plunger pot. Pump the plunger (top part) up and down in the pot for several minutes, as if using a butter churn. The milk will expand in volume by three to four times, creating froth for cappuccinos and lattes.

Disadvantages

The coffee may be cooled down by the time it has finished steeping. If the coffee grind is too fine, there may be difficulty in pressing down the plunger lid because of increased surface tension. Fine coffee sediment will remain at the bottom of the cup if a medium to coarse grind is not used. Extra cleanup is required, as this kind of pot has no paper filter.

The Vacuum Pot Method

This is the most dramatic and a unique way of preparing an excellent, full-flavored cup of coffee. Two glass globes, one set into another, with a filter, are suspended over a heat source. The setup looks more like a magical kerosene lamp than it does a coffeepot. Its sophisticated and attractive appeal was fashionable around the First World War and then again during the sixties and seventies. However, vacuum pots have lost much of their popularity, mainly due to their finicky and peculiar method.

The method

Place the pot's cloth filter in the upper funnel, and the ground coffee in the top glass globe. The coffee sits loosely around the filter, and the top is left open. Set the lower globe on its stand and fill it with boiling water from a kettle (if you wait for the small flame beneath the pot to boil the water, it will take hours). Fit the upper globe tightly upon the base, creating an airtight seal with the lower globe, and light the stand's low flame. Steam pressure will force the boiling water upward through the tube into the upper globe, where the water will begin to infuse the ground coffee. Stir the mixture, and allow the coffee to steep for 1 to 2 minutes, then turn off the flame. As the lower globe cools and contracts, a vacuum will form, and will suck the coffee down into the lower globe. When all the coffee has filtered down, remove the upper globe and pour the finished brew. Your guests will be impressed by your chemistry talents!

Brewing tips

To help speed up this method, boil the water separately in a kettle, then pour it into the lower globe and light the vacuum pot's heat source to begin the steam-pressure process. Make certain the entire brewing process is complete before removing the top globe.

Advantages

If you enjoy the theatrics of making an exotic brew, this method is impressive and entertaining. The pot is portable, and can be taken anywhere without any worry about electrical outlets. This method delivers an excellent, pure, fine coffee using a classic pot with cloth filters.

Disadvantages

This method is very time consuming. You definitely have to "go with the flow" with this one, since steam pressure is the driving force. The coffee brewing process must be absolutely complete before the top globe is removed. Patience and timing are crucial because if the top is removed too soon, the coffee will spill all over. Plastic models produce a muddy-looking brown coffee. The vacuum pot is a finicky and complex device.

The Middle Eastern Method

Each Mideastern country has its own variations of this method, such as Turkish or Greek coffee; however, all the techniques are similar in that very finely ground coffee is boiled with water and perhaps also sugar. This method produces a very heavy bodied, somewhat syrupy brew.

The method

A coffeepot called an ibrik (Turkish) or briki (Greek) is used. This is a long-handled copper or brass pot with a wide base and narrow top. For two servings: Place 2 heaping teaspoons (13 g) of powder-fine coffee in the pot along with 1/2 cup (125 ml) water and 2 heaping teaspoons (13 g) of sugar. Bring to a boil. When the coffee foams, remove the pot from the heat source; let the froth subside; stir. Repeat this heating process twice to produce a thick, black, muddy brew. Then pour the coffee into two 2-ounce (60 ml) cups. The grounds should be allowed to settle before the coffee is carefully consumed.

Brewing tips

Never fill the ibrik to more than half its capacity. The coffee foams lavishly and the pot must accommodate this expansion. Otherwise, it will spill over. When the coffee foams and is about to boil over, remove the pot from the stove and pour a bit of the foam into the serving cups. The traditional custom is to pour the coffee immediately to ensure that everyone receives equal amounts of foam and coffee grounds. Some people may prefer to have the grounds settle in the ibrik first, but this thick, sweet coffee has a tradition and taste all of its own, which requires serving the grounds along with the liquid coffee. For spiced variations, add cardamom seeds, cinnamon, nutmeg, or cloves to the pot while the coffee is boiling. In the Middle East, the usual proportion of sweetener is equal parts sugar and ground coffee; however, this can be increased or decreased to suit personal preferences.

Advantages

Once the grounds have settled, this heavy coffee is surprisingly mild and sweet if enough sugar has been added to it. The brewing process may be impressive and entertaining for guests.

Disadvantages

Producing a thin head of brown foam on the surface of the coffee is authentic to Middle Eastern coffee methods. However, it is not always achieved by a novice, so it may require some practice. People unused to this method may find the presence of coffee grounds in their cup disturbing to their coffee-drinking enjoyment. This brewing method requires a special, fine grind that is not advisable to attempt at home. If the coffee has not been pulverized sufficiently, the method will fail. It may not be easy to find the correct coffee and pot locally, and may be costly to order over the Internet.

The Percolator Method

In my opinion, boiled coffee is spoiled coffee. However, percolator-brewed coffee was quite popular during the 1930s and '40s. In this method, boiling water is force-pumped upward through a tube into a basket of ground coffee, literally boiling the coffee. Such pots drive away the delicate coffee aromatics and produce an overextracted, bitter brew.

The method

Fill the percolator with cold water. Place the ground coffee in the filter basket and insert the basket into the percolator. Cover and either place on a lit stove burner or if it is electric, plug it in. The heated water will create a steam pressure that forces it up through the coffee basket. The water repeatedly circulates over the bed of ground coffee, six to eight times, as the pot makes its characteristic bubbling sound.

Brewing tips

Use only coffee that has been coarsely ground.

Advantages

Its comforting aroma evokes a nostalgic memory of the catchy morning coffee music from television serials of the '50s.

Disadvantages

The delicate coffee aromatics and oils are burnt off, and the coffee achieved with this method is offensively distasteful and overextracted. Although there are various percolator styles and models to choose from, all of them produce bitter, lukewarm coffee. Medical research reports have consistently associated percolated coffee with high cholesterol issues.

Tips For Making The Perfect Cup Of Coffee

Perfection is purely a personal choice. No matter how good a person thinks a coffee is, your own palate is certainly "the best judge of the better java," as far as your own preferences go. Whether you are taking the coffee straight up or immersing it in a lofty lather of frothed milk, there are certain freshness fundamentals that will perk up (not percolate, heaven forbid!) your coffee and make it live up to its aromatic and flavorsome potential. Every ingredient should be the best, the freshest; and every technique should be performed properly to ensure a perfect beverage. Of course, the best coffee teacher is practice, practice, practice!

Clean equipment

If sediments remain in equipment after use, the odors can be absorbed, and the remaining coffee oils can turn rancid, which will take a serious toll on future brews. Baking soda mixed with warm water is a great cleaning agent for nonpaper filters, coffeemakers, carafes, and cups (a pastelike solution of this will safely scrub coffee stains from even your finest china).

Fresh water

Try not to use tap water for coffeemaking. The dissolved base minerals in hard water can cause a damaging buildup of hardened mineral and calcium deposits that can clog the fine steam and water channels inside your equipment. Chlorine-free, filtered or distilled water is most preferable (even carbon-filtered tap water is better than plain tap water), as these are free of any flavor or unfavorable odor that might distort the taste of your coffee. If you get water from the tap, start with cold water, because it hasn't been sitting in the pipes or the boiler for a long time. Whether to use softened water is a personal choice. Some people do not mind it; others say the phosphates and other agents in soft water produce a soapy-tasting coffee.

Proper grind and brewing time

The correct grind and length of brewing (contact) time the coffee requires varies according to the brewing method.

Proper quantities

A standard rule when using a fine coffee grind is 1 tablespoon (15 ml) ground coffee per 8-ounce (250 ml) cup of water. If a double-strength brew is preferred, use 1 rounded tablespoon (22 ml) per 1/2 cup (4 ounces [125 ml]) of water. If using a coarser grind, for example, as many as 4 rounded tablespoons (88 ml) per 2 1/2 cups (20 ounces [625 ml]) of water may be used. The most important rule here is: follow your own taste. This is a very personal choice.

Proper temperature

When you boil water separately in a kettle, it should come to a full, rolling boil (212°F [100°C] at sea level, slightly less at higher altitudes), not merely a simmer. The correct water temperature is 195° to 205°F (90° to 96°C) when the water is in contact with the ground coffee, and should be 185° to 190°F (85° to 88°C) when the coffee has finished brewing. When using an electrical device, a good reference is the wattage on the coffeemaker: the higher the wattage, the more powerful the heater, and the better the coffee should be. Preferably, the machine will rate over 1,000 watts; however, most home machines are around 850 watts.

Recipes

Coffee Syrup

This versatile syrup is perfect for making iced coffees. It is also great for desserts and over ice cream, too! Yield: about 1 cup (250 ml)

Ingredients

- 2 cups (500 ml) hot, fresh espresso or strong coffee

- 1 1/3 cups (350 g) sugar

- 1 vanilla bean, split lengthwise
- 1/3 cup (75 ml) dark roast coffee beans, cracked slightly
- A pinch of salt

Directions

- Combine the espresso, sugar, vanilla bean, coffee beans, and salt in a medium-size saucepan.
- Cook over low heat, stirring frequently, until the sugar is dissolved.
- Bring to a boil over medium-high heat and cook, without stirring, for about 4 minutes, or until thick and syrupy.
- Remove the saucepan from the heat and let cool completely.
- Strain the espresso mixture through a fine sieve into a small bowl.
- Discard the coffee beans and, if desired, set the vanilla bean aside for another use.
- Cover the syrup with plastic wrap and chill until ready to use. The syrup can be kept refrigerated for up to 1 month.

Espresso Syrup

Another handy flavoring to have in the kitchen, it is also easy to prepare. This rich syrup can be used as a sweet flavoring in iced coffees (or on waffles, pancakes, or ice cream, too!). Yield: 1 cup (250 ml)

Ingredients

- 3/4 cup (165 g) granulated sugar or vanilla sugar

- 1/4 cup (60 ml) water

- 4 ounces (113 ml) hot, fresh espresso or strong coffee

Directions

- Combine the sugar and water in a small saucepan, and bring to a boil. Lower the heat and simmer for 5 minutes.

- Remove from the heat and let cool for 1 minute.

- Stir in the espresso.

- Allow the syrup to sit for at least 30 minutes before using.

- Store the syrup in a sealed jar in the refrigerator. It will keep for several weeks (if you don't tell anyone it's there!).

Chocolate Syrup
Yield: 2 1/2 cups (625 ml)

Ingredients

- 1 1/2 cups (330 g) sugar
- 1 cup (220 g) sifted unsweetened cocoa powder
- A pinch of salt
- 1 cup (250 ml) water
- 2 teaspoons (10 ml) vanilla extract

Directions

- Combine the sugar, cocoa powder, and salt in a saucepan.
- Whisk thoroughly.
- Gradually add the water to the cocoa, stirring (not beating) with the whisk to blend thoroughly.
- Place over medium heat, stirring frequently with the whisk until the mixture comes to a boil. A layer of foam may form on top of the syrup.
- Boil for 3 minutes, stirring constantly with the whisk. Reduce the heat if the syrup threatens to boil over.
- Remove from the heat; pour into a heatproof liquid measuring cup (3 cup/750 ml capacity).

- Let cool briefly, then chill, uncovered, in the refrigerator until completely cold.

- Strain through a fine strainer into a 2 1/2-cup (625 ml) container.

- Stir in the vanilla.

- Store, covered, in the refrigerator. The syrup can be kept refrigerated for up to 2 weeks.

Vanilla Whipped Cream

This one's a keeper! Here is a traditional European recipe I learned from Tante Maria. Yield: about 3 cups (750 ml)

Ingredients

- 2 cups (500 ml) chilled whipping cream (35 percent milk fat)

- 3 tablespoons (43 g) vanilla sugar, or purchase commercially prepared

Directions

- Whip the cream with an electric mixer on medium speed until soft peaks form.

- Add the vanilla sugar, 1 tablespoon (14 g) at a time.

- Do not overbeat.

- Serve immediately or store in the refrigerator for up to 4 hours before serving.

Espresso Whipped Cream
Yield: about 2 cups (500 ml)

Ingredients

- 1 cup (250 ml) chilled whipping cream

- 3 tablespoons (43 g) light brown sugar

- 1 teaspoon (5 ml) vanilla extract

- 1 teaspoon (3 g) instant espresso powder

Directions

- Whip all the ingredients in a medium-size, chilled bowl until soft peaks form.

- Serve immediately, or store in the refrigerator until needed.

Coffee Liqueur Whipped Cream
Absolutely fabulous on any coffee cocktail! Yield: 2 cups (500 ml)

Ingredients

- 1 cup (250 ml) chilled whipping cream
- 1/2 cup (110 g) sifted confectioners' sugar
- 3 tablespoons (45 ml) coffee syrup or coffee-flavored liqueur

Directions

- Whip the whipping cream in a chilled mixing bowl until foamy.
- Gradually add the sugar.
- Whip until soft peaks form.
- Fold in the syrup.
- Cover and chill until ready to serve.

Chocolate Whipped Cream

A chocolate-lover's topping for mochaccinos, or for a plain cup of joe. Yield: 2 to 2 1/2 cups (500 to 625 ml)

Ingredients

- 1 cup (250 ml) chilled whipping cream
- 3 tablespoons (43 g) confectioners' sugar

- 2 tablespoons (28 g) semisweet cocoa powder
- 1/2 teaspoon (2 ml) crème de cacao syrup or liqueur

Directions

- Whip the cream in a chilled bowl, using an electric mixer, until soft peaks form.
- Fold in the dry ingredients 1 tablespoon (15 ml) at a time.
- Fold in the crème de cacao syrup.
- Chill for 30 minutes before using.

Coffee Whipped Cream

This is wonderful to use on any coffee cocktail or specialty coffee. Yield: about 1 cup (250 ml)

Ingredients

- 1/2 cup (125 ml) chilled whipping cream
- 2 tablespoons (28 g) sugar
- 1 tablespoon (14 g) instant coffee

Directions

- Whip the cream with the sugar and instant coffee.

- Chill for at least 3 hours.
- Whip again until peaks form.
- Serve immediately.

Cinnamon Whipped Cream

Simply great for all coffee- and cinnamon-lovers! Yield: approximately 2 cups (500 ml)

Ingredients

- 1 cup (250 ml) chilled whipping cream
- 3 tablespoons (43 g) confectioners' sugar
- 1 teaspoon (3 g) ground cinnamon

Directions

- Combine all the ingredients in a chilled mixing bowl.
- Whip until soft peaks form.
- Chill until ready to serve.

Soy Whipped Cream

The alternative whipped cream! Yield: about 1 cup (250 ml)

Ingredients

- 1/4 cup (60 ml) soy milk
- 1/2 cup (125 ml) vegetable oil
- 1 tablespoon (15 ml) real maple syrup
- 1/2 teaspoon (2 ml) vanilla extract

Directions

- Place the soy milk and 1/4 cup (60 ml) of the oil in a blender.
- Blend at highest speed and slowly drizzle in the remaining 1/4 cup (60 ml) oil.
- Blend in the maple syrup and vanilla, adding a little more oil if necessary to thicken.
- Serve immediately to top coffee beverages or your favorite dessert.

Be Mine Latte
From the coffee cherry of my heart!

Ingredients

- 1 ounce (60 ml) premium gourmet black cherry syrup

- 1 1/2 ounces (45 ml) hot, fresh espresso or strong coffee

- 8 ounces (250 ml) steamed milk

- Whipped cream, for garnish

- 1 maraschino cherry, for garnish

Directions

- Mix the syrup, espresso, and milk together in a tempered glass coffee mug.

- Top with whipped cream and a cherry.

French Kiss Caffè Latte

Dedicated to my "French-Swiss" soulmate—Bobbie. Serves 2

Ingredients

- 1/2-ounce (15 ml) vanilla-flavored syrup, Irish cream liqueur or coffee flavored liqueur

- 1/2-ounce (15 ml) caramel syrup or orange-flavored liqueur

- 4 ounces (113 ml) steamed milk

- 2 ounces (60 ml) hot, fresh espresso or strong coffee

- Whipped cream, for garnish

Directions

- Pour the syrups into two stemmed tempered glass mugs.

- Add the steamed milk, but do not stir.

- Add the espresso to the milk mixture.

- Top with a dollop of whipped cream.

- Serve with a kiss.

Love Potion Latte
For the love of lattes! Serves 2

Ingredients

- 1-ounce (30 ml) orange-flavored syrup or liqueur

- 1-ounce (30 ml) hazelnut-flavored syrup or liqueur

- 4 ounces (113 ml) hot, fresh espresso or strong coffee

- 8 ounces (250 ml) milk

- Cocoa powder, for garnish

- Ground cinnamon, for garnish

Directions

- Pour the syrups into two 12–ounce (340 ml) latte mugs.

- Pour the hot espresso into the cups.

- Steam the milk until it has almost doubled in volume.

- Dollop the frothed milk into the cups.

- Dust with cocoa or cinnamon and serve immediately.

Irish Elixir Espresso
An old-fashioned coffee cure-all.

Ingredients

- 2 ounces (60 ml) premium gourmet peppermint-flavored syrup

- 1 ounce (30 ml) premium gourmet chocolate syrup

- 1 1/2 ounces (45 ml) hot, fresh espresso or strong coffee

- 8 ounces (250 ml) steamed milk

Directions

- Pour all the ingredients into an Irish coffee mug.

- Stir, and enjoy!

Iced Irish Coffee

Lips will stay stuck in the sipping position! Serves 2

Ingredients

- 3 ounces (90 ml) B-52 syrup or coffee-flavored liqueur
- 1/2 teaspoon (2 ml) vanilla extract
- 2 tablespoons (30 g) sugar
- 6–8 ounces (170–250 ml) cold espresso or strong coffee
- A few ice cubes
- Whipped cream, for garnish

Directions

- Stir the syrup, vanilla, and sugar into the cold coffee.
- Fill two tall glasses with ice cubes and the cold coffee mixture.
- Top with mounds of whipped cream.

Shamrock Shimmy (Nonskinny) Latte

Lucky leprechauns love this latte!

Ingredients

- 1 1/2 ounces (45 ml) premium gourmet peppermint-flavored syrup

- 1 ounce (30 ml) premium gourmet cookie dough syrup

- 1/2 ounce (15 ml) premium gourmet chocolate syrup

- 1 1/2 ounces (45 ml) hot, fresh espresso or strong coffee

- 8 ounces (250 ml) steamed milk

Directions

- Mix all the syrups together in an Irish coffee mug.

- Add the hot coffee to the blended syrups.

- Pour the steamed milk into the mug.

Seven-Layer Latte

Halloween latte lovers will howl—this is as much fun to drink as it is to make!

Ingredients

- 10 ounces (310 ml) milk

- 1-ounce (30 ml) orange-flavored syrup

- 1 1/2 ounces (45 ml) chocolate syrup

- 1-ounce (30 ml) hazelnut-flavored syrup

- 2–3 ounces (60–85 ml) hot, fresh espresso or strong coffee

- Cocoa powder, for garnish

- Black and orange sprinkles, for garnish

Directions

- Steam the milk in a saucepan with a flexible, loose wired whisk or hand-mixer, or with a steam wand from an espresso machine.

- In a cup, mix 3 ounces (85 ml) of the milk with the orange-flavored syrup, to produce orange foam.

- In a separate cup, mix 3 ounces (85 ml) of the milk with 1 ounce (30 ml) of the chocolate syrup and 1/2 ounce (15 ml) of the hazelnut flavored syrup, to produce tan colored foam.

- Into a clear, tall, tapered tempered 16- ounce (250 ml) glass:

  ☐ LAYER 1: Pour 1/2 ounce (15 ml) of the chocolate syrup.

☐ LAYER 2: Pour 1/2 ounce (15 ml) of the hazelnutflavored syrup.

☐ LAYER 3: Very slowly pour or spoon 2 ounces (60 ml) of the untinted milk.

☐ LAYER 4: Very slowly pour or spoon 3 ounces (45 ml) of the orange-colored milk.

☐ LAYER 5: Very slowly pour or spoon 3 ounces (45 ml) of the tan-colored milk.

☐ LAYER 6: Very slowly pour or spoon the remaining 2 ounces (60 ml) untinted milk.

☐ LAYER 7: Very slowly pour the espresso down the center of the entire layered drink. (Important: As you pour in the espresso, keep the drink still so the coffee will create buoyant, separated, colorful layers like magic!)

• Dust with cocoa powder.

• Garnish with orange and black sprinkles.

Thanksgiving Orange Latte
You'll be grateful for this yummy drink!

Ingredients

- 3/4-ounce (20 ml) orange-flavored syrup or liqueur
- 1/4-ounce (7 ml) amaretto or almond-flavored syrup
- 2 ounces (60 ml) hot, fresh espresso or strong coffee
- 6–8 ounces (170–250 ml) steamed half-and-half
- Whipped cream, for garnish
- Orange sprinkles, for garnish

Directions

- Pour the syrup and amaretto into a 12–ounce (340 ml) latte or cappuccino mug.
- Add the espresso to the mug.
- Scoop the steamed half-and-half onto the top of the drink.
- Top with whipped cream and orange sprinkles.

Pumpkin Cheesecake Latte

A delicious liquid pumpkin dessert.

Ingredients

- 1/2 ounce (15 ml) premium gourmet cheesecake syrup
- 1/2 ounce (15 ml) premium gourmet pumpkin spice syrup

- 8 ounces (250 ml) milk

- 1 1/2–3 ounces (45–90 ml) hot, fresh espresso or strong coffee

Directions

- Steam the syrups and milk until hot, frothy, and doubled in volume.

- Pour into a tempered 12-ounce (340 ml) glass.

- Pour the hot espresso into the milk mixture.

- Top with a layer of frothed milk.

Happy Holiday Coffee Punch
A yummy crowd-pleaser. Serves 35

Ingredients

- 1 cup (250 ml) whipping cream

- 1/4 teaspoon (1.2 g) salt

- 1/2 cup (110 g) sugar

- 1/4 teaspoon (1 ml) almond extract

- 1/2 teaspoon (2 ml) vanilla extract

- 1 quart (1 L) cold strong coffee

- 1-quart (.95 L) vanilla ice cream

- 1-quart (.95 L) chocolate ice cream

- 1/2 teaspoon (1.5 g) grated nutmeg

- 1/4 teaspoon (1.2 g) ground cinnamon

Directions

- Whip the whipping cream in a bowl, slowly adding the salt, sugar, and almond and vanilla extracts.

- Pour the chilled coffee into a punch bowl.

- Add walnut-size chunks of ice cream to the punch bowl.

- Fold the whipped cream into the punch.

- Sprinkle with nutmeg and cinnamon.

Orange Yule Delight Latte
"Yule" glow with delight as you serve this!

Ingredients

- 4 ounces (113 ml) light cream or milk

- 2 ounces (60 ml) hot, fresh espresso or strong coffee

- 3/4-ounce (20 ml) orange-flavored syrup or liqueur

- 1/4-ounce (7 ml) amaretto or almond-flavored syrup

Directions

- Steam the light cream until hot, frothy, and doubled in volume.

- Pour into a mug.

- Pour the hot espresso, syrup, and amaretto into the frothy cream and stir gently.

Christmas Cappuccino
Christmas à la crème.

Ingredients

- 4 ounces (113 ml) eggnog

- 2 ounces (60 ml) hot, fresh espresso or strong coffee

- 1/2-ounce (15 ml) sambuca (optional)

- 1/2 ounce (15 ml) premium egg yolk liqueur (optional)

- Whipped cream, for garnish

- Ground cinnamon, for garnish

- Grated nutmeg, for garnish

- 1 cinnamon stick, for stirring

Directions

- Steam the eggnog until it has doubled in volume.

- Pour the eggnog into a tempered Christmas glass or mug.

- Gently pour the espresso down the side of the glass into the eggnog.

- If using the liqueurs, gently pour them into the finished beverage.

- Scoop a dollop of whipped cream onto the top.

- Dust with cinnamon and nutmeg.

- Serve immediately, with the cinnamon stick.

Snowflake Latte
Mint lovers will melt away with this latte!

Ingredients

- 1/2 ounce (15 ml) premium gourmet vanilla-flavored syrup

- 1/2 ounce (15 ml) premium gourmet peppermint-flavored syrup

- 1 1/2 ounces (45 ml) hot, fresh espresso or strong coffee

- 10 ounces (310 ml) steamed milk

Directions

- Combine all the ingredients in a coffee mug, and stir.

- Enjoy!

Classic Christmas Coffee

A merry coffee to warm the whiskers with!

Ingredients

- 1 1/2 ounces (45 ml) premium whiskey or rye

- 2 1/2 teaspoons (8.25 ml) real maple syrup

- 3/4 cup (176 ml) hot, fresh espresso or strong coffee

- 1/4 cup (30 ml) whipping cream (unwhipped), for garnish

- 1 candy cane, for garnish

Directions

- Combine the whiskey and 1 1/2 teaspoons (7 ml) of the maple syrup in a heated mug or cup.

- Fill the rest of the way with the coffee.

- In a small bowl, combine the whipping cream with the remaining 1 teaspoon (1.25 ml) maple syrup, and whip until soft peaks form.

- Spoon the flavored whipped cream on top of the coffee mixture.

- Top with the candy cane!

Candy Cane Latte
This drink will spread Christmas cheer.

Ingredients

- 3/4-ounce (20 ml) cherry-flavored syrup or kirsch

- 1/4-ounce (7 ml) crème de menthe syrup or liqueur

- 2 ounces (30 ml) hot, fresh espresso or strong coffee

- 4–6 ounces (113–170 ml) steamed milk

- Whipped cream, for garnish

- Small candy canes, for garnish

Directions

- Pour the syrups and espresso into a 12–ounce (340 ml) latte mug.

- Add the steamed milk.

- Top with whipped cream.

- Garnish with small candy canes hanging off the rim of the mug.

Midnight Star Coffee Cocktail

A starry coffee spirit to settle back with!

Ingredients

- 1 1/2 ounces (45 ml) hot, fresh espresso or strong coffee

- 1 1/2 ounces (45 ml) hazelnut flavored syrup

- 1 1/2 ounces (45 ml) vanilla flavored vodka

- 4 ounces (125 ml) crushed ice

- Whipped cream, for garnish

- Cocoa powder, for garnish

Directions

- Place the espresso, syrup, vodka, and ice in a cocktail shaker.

- Shake vigorously—the hot espresso will melt the ice and dilute all the ingredients rapidly, and the mixture should be nice and frothy.

- Strain into a chilled glass.

- Float the whipped cream on top.

- Garnish with cocoa powder in a "star-dusting" fashion.

CPSIA information can be obtained
at www.ICGtesting.com
Printed in the USA
LVHW030155170223
739736LV00014B/775